It's Laugh O'Clock
Would You Rather?
Thanksgiving Edition

Funny Scenarios, Wacky Choices
and Hilarious Situations
For Kids and Family

With Fun Illustrations

Riddleland

Copyright 2021 - Riddleland All rights reserved.

The content contained within this book may not be reproduced, duplicated, or transmitted without direct written permission from the author or the publisher.

By reading this document, the reader agrees that under no circumstances is the author responsible for any losses, direct or indirect, that are incurred due to the use of the information contained within this document, including, but not limited to, errors, omissions, or inaccuracies.

Legal Notice:
This book is copyright protected. It is only for personal use. You cannot amend, distribute, sell, use, quote, or paraphrase any part, or the content within this book, without the author or publisher's consent.

Disclaimer Notice:
Please note the information contained within this document is for educational and entertainment purposes only. All effort has been executed to present accurate, up to date, reliable, complete information. No warranties of any kind are declared or implied. Readers acknowledge that the author is not engaged in the rendering of legal, financial, medical, or professional advice. The content within this book has been derived from various sources. Please consult a licensed professional before attempting any techniques outlined in this book.

Designs by freepik.com

TABLE OF CONTENTS

Introduction   pg   5

Turn it into a game   pg   7

Would You Rather?   pg   9

Did you enjoy the book?   pg 108

Bonus Book   pg 109

Contest   pg 110

Other books by Riddleland   pg 111

About Riddleland   pg 113

Riddleland Bonus

Join our **Facebook Group** at **Riddleland for Kids** to get daily jokes and riddles.

• • • • • • • • • • • • • • • • • • • •

https://pixelfy.me/riddlelandbonus

Thank you for buying this book. As a token of our appreciation, we would like to offer a special bonus—a collection of 50 original jokes, riddles, and funny stories.

INTRODUCTION

"Gratitude unlocks the fullness of life. It turns what we have into enough."
~ Melody Beattle

Are you ready to make some decisions? **It's Laugh O'Clock - Would You Rather? Thanksgiving Edition** is a collection of funny scenarios, wacky choices, and hilarious situations which offer alternative endings for kids and adults to choose among.

These questions are an excellent way to get a fun and exciting conversation started. Also, by asking "Why?" after a "Would you Rather . . . " question, learn a lot about the person, including their values and their thinking process.

We wrote this book because we want children to be encouraged to read more, think, and grow. As parents, we know that when children play games, they are being educated while having so much fun that they don't even realize they're learning and developing valuable life skills. "Would you Rather . . . " is one of our favorite games to play as a family. Some of the 'would you rather ...' scenarios have had us in fits of giggles, others have generated reactions such as: "Eeeeeeuuugh, that's gross!" and yet others really make us think, reflect and consider our own decisions.

Besides having fun, playing these questions have other benefits such as:

Enhancing Communication – This game helps children to interact, read aloud, and listen to others. It's a fun way for parents to get their children interacting with them without a formal, awkward conversation. The game can also help to get to know someone better and learn about their likes, dislikes, and values.

Building Confidence – The game encourages children to get used to pronouncing vocabulary, asking questions, and overcoming shyness.

Developing Critical Thinking – It helps children to defend and justify the rationale for their choices and can generate discussions and debates. Parents playing this game with young children can give them prompting questions about their answers to help them reach logical and sensible decisions.

Improving Vocabulary – Children will be introduced to new words in the questions, and the context of them will help them remember the words because the game is fun.

Encouraging Equality and Diversity – Considering other people's answers, even if they differ from your own, is important for respect, equality, diversity, tolerance, acceptance, and inclusivity. Some questions may get children to think outside the box and move beyond stereotypes associated with gender.

Welcome to It's Laugh O'Clock

Would You Rather?
Thanksgiving Edition

How do you play?

At least two players are needed to play this game. Face your opponent and decide who is **Turkey 1** and **Turkey 2**. If you have 3 or 4 players, you can decide which players belong to **Turkey Group 1** and **Turkey Group 2**. The goal of the game is to score points by making the other players laugh. The first player to a score of 10 points is the **Round Champion**.

What are the rules?

Turkey 1 starts first. Read the questions aloud and choose an answer. The same player will then explain why they chose the answer in the silliest and wackiest way possible. If the reason makes the Turkey 2 laugh, then Turkey 1 scores a funny point. Take turns going back and forth and write down the score.

If you have three or four players

Flip a coin. The Turkey that guesses it correctly starts first.

Bonus Tip:
Making funny voices, silly dance moves or wacky facial expressions will make your opponent laugh!

Most Importantly:

Remember to have fun and enjoy the game!

Would You Rather...

Eat a turkey that is still raw

eat a pumpkin pie with a soggy crust and runny filling that is not fully baked?

Eat the entire Thanksgiving dinner using only your hands, including the cranberries,

eat the entire dinner without using your hands?

Would You Rather...

Have a snowball fight using
sticky clumps of mashed potatoes

have a water fight using cranberry sauce?

Have your lawn chair break in half while you're sitting
on it around the bonfire

have a black crow fly by and poop on your head?

Would You Rather...

Eat Thanksgiving dinner out of your dog's food bowl

only be able to eat the scraps and crumbs that your family drops onto the floor during the meal?

Eat your mashed potatoes topped with a cranberry-flavored gravy

eat a bowl of stuffing that has tons of liver and onions?

Would You Rather...

Eat Thanksgiving dinner surrounded by snow and ice in Antarctica

surrounded by palm trees on a tropical island?

Spill a cup of hot chocolate all over your shoes so they squish whenever you take a step

have scratchy straw in your socks so it keeps scraping your ankles whenever you take a step?

 ## Would You Rather...

Accidentally drop and break one of your mom's special china plates

accidentally break your drinking glass and get a piece of it stuck in your finger when you try to clean it up?

Eat Thanksgiving dinner with only your teacher and classmates at school

only with your family at home, no guests allowed?

Would You Rather...

Be in charge of cooking the entire
Thanksgiving meal by yourself

do everyone's dinner dishes all by yourself?

Rather rake and gather up
twenty big bags of fallen leaves for $5

pay a friend $10 to rake up the
twenty big bags of fallen leaves?

 # Would You Rather...

Have the flu on Thanksgiving and miss getting to eat dinner with the family

have the flu on Christmas and miss getting to open your presents with the family?

Eat Thanksgiving dinner served up by your school's cafeteria lunch ladies

outside on a giant picnic table on a breezy day?

 ## Would You Rather...

Wear just a tablecloth to Thanksgiving dinner with your family

a fancy outfit that is two sizes too tight?

Find a piece of pumpkin shell baked into your pumpkin pie

eat a spoonful of really really lumpy mashed potatoes?

 ## Would You Rather...

Peel potatoes using only your teeth

eat turkey that has already been chewed up by someone else?

Be able to use your mashed potatoes in place of your school glue bottle

paint a masterpiece using only a bowl of cooked cranberries?

Would You Rather...

Have teeth that are the color of turkey gravy

eyes that are the color of cranberries?

Eat a bowl of tart cranberries that have no added sugar and taste like lemons

eat a whole bowl of mashed turnips buried in a pool of gravy?

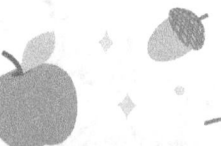

Would You Rather...

Eat just meat (meaning only turkey)

eat only vegetables (mashed potatoes, yams, green bean casserole) for Thanksgiving dinner?

Catch the winning football game touchdown, but get tackled in the end zone and barf up your dinner

drop the ball instead of scoring the winning touchdown and have everyone ignore you for the rest of the day?

Would You Rather...

Get super wrinkly fingers from doing the family's Thanksgiving dishes

burn your fingers helping your dad carve the Thanksgiving turkey?

Sit next to your uncle who always unbuttons his pants halfway through the meal

next to your little brother or sister who always burps loudly during the meal?

Would You Rather...

Scoop all your Thanksgiving food onto your plate using only your hands

mash the potatoes by stepping on them with your bare feet?

Spend your afternoon pulling little turkey bits off the turkey

spend your morning peeling potatoes to make mashed potatoes?

Would You Rather...

Eat sweet potatoes made by your grandma that are just white potatoes with a bunch of sugar

eat rolls made by your mom that are super hard and crusty and coated in butter?

Have to eat the scraps of food off someone else's plate

have to switch silverware with someone else after they've started eating?

Would You Rather...

Choke on a piece of turkey during dinner and end up spitting half-chewed turkey all over everyone's food

have to eat everything on your plate after your grandma sneezes all over your food?

Fish your grandma's pair of fake teeth out of her glass of apple juice

go into the bathroom after your grandpa used it and didn't turn on the fan?

 # Would You Rather...

Accidentally pass gas loudly while your family is giving thanks before the meal

snort apple juice out of your nose when your dad tells a funny joke during the meal?

Use pumpkin pie scented shampoo and conditioner

wash your hair using a can of pumpkin pie filling?

 ## Would You Rather...

Get caught passing green beans under the table to your dog

get caught kicking your little brother or sister under the table?

Sleep all night with a bare tree branch tapping on your window

with a chipper owl "hoo'ing" through the night right outside your window?

Would You Rather...

Dress up in a giant turkey costume that makes you super sweaty

have real turkey feathers glued all over your body?

Go on a hayride with a really gassy and smelly horse pulling you

go on a hayride sitting next to someone who babbles nonstop the entire time?

Would You Rather...

Have a pet fish cracker called Cranberry floating in a fishbowl next to your bed

a pet potato called Spud you drag on a leash everywhere you go?

Make a snow fort out of a giant pile of mashed potatoes

dig a snow tunnel through a big stack of mashed yams?

 ## Would You Rather...

Have everyone say one thing they're grateful for all at the same time before the meal

have to go one by one and say something you're grateful for before you can eat?

Climb a tree and jump off it into a giant pile of dry crunchy leaves

onto a bunch of stacked square hay bales?

Would You Rather...

Eat Thanksgiving dinner restaurant style with you being the waiter or waitress

buffet style where everyone lines up to serve their own food - starting with oldest to youngest?

Have a new rule that kids eat last at Thanksgiving

kids eat first but only get to eat the food that their parents put on their plates?

Would You Rather...

Grow a pig's tail and a snout if you eat a second helping at Thanksgiving dinner

have your stomach blow up like a big balloon if you eat a second helping?

Eat a giant bowl of yucky orange pumpkin soup

drink a cranberry green bean casserole smoothie?

 ## Would You Rather...

Switch plates of food with
your grandpa

your younger brother or sister?

Hold hands with someone's hot and sweaty hand while
giving thanks

have someone hold your hand so tightly that
it goes numb?

Would You Rather...

Make a sandcastle out of goopy mashed potatoes

eat a mashed potato sandcastle sculpted by your little brother or sister's dirty hands?

Eat a pumpkin pie made from sweet potatoes

a Thanksgiving chicken instead of a turkey?

Would You Rather...

Eat so much that you pass out during dinner and your face lands in a plateful of mashed yams

in a giant gravy bowl?

Look around the table and see that everyone has at least one piece of food stuck to their face that they don't know about

have a piece of food stuck to your face that you don't know about and no one tells you about?

Would You Rather...

Be so hungry at dinner time that you stuff a whole bunch of steaming hot food in your face and badly burn your mouth

have to wait so long for everyone to give thanks before eating that your food is ice cold by the time you get to eat?

Bob for apples
in a giant tub of jellied cranberries

in a giant tub of buttery mashed yams?

 ## Would You Rather...

Sit in a chair that is made for someone much smaller than you so you look huge on a tiny chair

have to share a chair with your brother or sister because you ran out of chairs to go around the table?

Lick your dad's plate clean after eating dinner

eat your dinner off a plate licked clean by your dog?

Would You Rather...

Eat pumpkin pie baked in a raw pumpkin shell

eat a pumpkin pie topped with whipped mashed potatoes instead of whipped cream?

Eat a bag of potato chips instead of mashed potatoes and gravy

a package of beef jerky instead of Thanksgiving turkey?

 ## Would You Rather...

Eat a pound of creamy yellow butter

drink a gallon of thick brown gravy?

Wake up at 5am to put the turkey in the oven on Thanksgiving

oversleep you and no one wakes you up in time to eat turkey dinner with the family?

Would You Rather...

Eat black and burned turkey
for Thanksgiving

have no turkey to eat on Thanksgiving?

Weave Thanksgiving dinner placemats for everyone
out of dried corn husks

gather 1,000 acorns to make a massive wreath
for your front door?

 ## Would You Rather...

Try to eat your dinner with swim flippers
on your hands

try to sip your drink with a duck's bill instead of a mouth?

Celebrate Thanksgiving by complaining about stuff
all day long instead of giving thanks

eat Thanksgiving dinner at a table where
no one can talk?

Would You Rather...

Have to babysit your younger siblings and cousins while the rest of the family plays games

get stuck listening to your half-deaf grandparent yell stories at you about their childhood?

Lick the person's fingers who sits next to you at dinner

have the person who sits next to you lick your fingers?

 # Would You Rather...

Eat Thanksgiving dinner standing at the table

sitting with your legs crossed on the floor because you don't have a chair?

Eat lima bean casserole because you're out of green beans

pumpkin pie made from squash because the store had sold out of canned pumpkin?

Would You Rather...

Take a bath in a big tub of melted butter

use a stick of butter to wash yourself instead of a bar of soap?

Go swimming in an outdoor pool on a crisp chilly fall day and get covered in goosebumps

be a kite that another kid is flying on a windy day?

 ## Would You Rather...

Be like Goldilocks and eat food that is way too hot

way too cold at Thanksgiving dinner?

Eat your entire Thanksgiving dinner blended into a smoothie

only be able to eat one kind of food all day on Thanksgiving Day?

Would You Rather...

Have your hair smell like stuffing made with chicken liver

your feet smell like turkey gravy for a week?

Be able to squirt sticky caramel out of your belly button

have the head of a sunflower that is filled with yummy sunflower seeds you can eat?

 # Would You Rather...

Run a Turkey Trot race (3.1 miles) dressed in a turkey ballerina tutu

run a Turkey Trot race right after eating Thanksgiving dinner?

Ask and answer gross "Would You Rather" questions with your family over dinner

hear the same old family stories you hear every year while you eat dinner?

Would You Rather...

Have your cat jump up onto the table during dinner and run on top of all of the food

have your dog pull down the tablecloth and everything from the table onto the floor during dinner?

Drink a glass of boiled potato juice

eat cooked sweet potato skins?

Would You Rather...

Spend three hours Thanksgiving grocery shopping with your mom

write a list of one hundred things you are grateful for as a school project?

Eat sweet potatoes with a bunch of really hard marshmallows in them

mashed sweet potatoes that still have the skin on?

Would You Rather...

Have green beans from the casserole for eyebrows

slimy cranberries for eyeballs?

Have a cafeteria meal turkey dinner with lunch meat turkey sandwich slices instead of big juicy pieces of turkey

find out that the mashed potatoes they are serving are powdered flakes of potato with water added to them?

Would You Rather...

Eat Thanksgiving dinner out of take-out foam containers

use your little sister's doll-sized china tea set?

Get pumpkin pie crust crumbs all over the keyboard of your computer

mashed potatoes and gravy smeared all over the computer screen?

Would You Rather...

Bake the apple pie and forget to add sugar to it so there are just really sour apples baked into a crust

accidentally leave the vanilla ice cream on the counter so it is poured on top of your pie like gravy?

Eat a completely meat free Thanksgiving dinner

eat a Thanksgiving dinner that has meat in everything?

 # Would You Rather...

Sit next to your bearded uncle at Thanksgiving and eat all of the crumbs that fall onto your plate off his beard

sit next to your aunt who keeps pinching and squeezing your cheeks all through the meal?

Build with Legos a cabin in the woods that you can live in

a boat that you can sail on the lake in?

Would You Rather...

Pour butter over everything you eat for Thanksgiving

eat your entire meal without using butter?

Eat a big stack of smoky turkey-flavored pancakes covered with gravy

a juicy pumpkin pie-flavored hamburger topped with whipped cream?

 # Would You Rather...

Show up to Thanksgiving dinner dressed as Santa Claus, complete with a big white fuzzy beard

as a plumped-up turkey, with giant tail feathers sticking out of your rear end?

Jump in a bouncy house made from roasted marshmallows

drive bumper cars in a rink made of jellied cranberries?

Would You Rather...

Only be able to eat foods that you have made for Thanksgiving dinner

only be able to eat food that matches the color of the outfit you are wearing to dinner?

Spill dark red cranberries all over your pants

sit in a pool of gravy that was spilled on your chair?

 ## Would You Rather...

Sit on a chair that has food smeared all over it

eat your meal off a dirty plate and with a dirty fork?

Scrape dried mashed potatoes and gravy from the bottom of school cafeteria tables

pick up squished green beans one by one with your fingers from the cafeteria floor?

Would You Rather...

Smuggle Thanksgiving leftovers into your pockets for later

smuggle leftovers into your socks for later?

Find a plate of week old Thanksgiving leftovers that you forgot about under your bed

find a big crusty blob of dried mashed potatoes in your belly button when you go to put on your pjs?

Would You Rather...

Captain a sailboat in an ocean of brown gravy

hike up a mountain of mashed potatoes?

Eat Thanksgiving dinner on a table that is really sticky so everything that touches it sticks to the table

on a table that is really slippery so the dishes and silverware keep sliding right off of the table?

Would You Rather...

Go to school like the Pilgrims,
and not be able to use pens, markers, and glue sticks

not be able to use computers?

Spend six hours driving to your family's
Thanksgiving celebration

spend six days preparing food for your family's
Thanksgiving celebration?

 # Would You Rather...

Cook your entire Thanksgiving dinner outside over a fire like the Pilgrims might have done

only be able to eat food for Thanksgiving that can be cooked in a microwave?

Have to sit on a chair seat made from sticky marshmallow fluff

sit on a seat made from lumpy pecan pie?

Would You Rather...

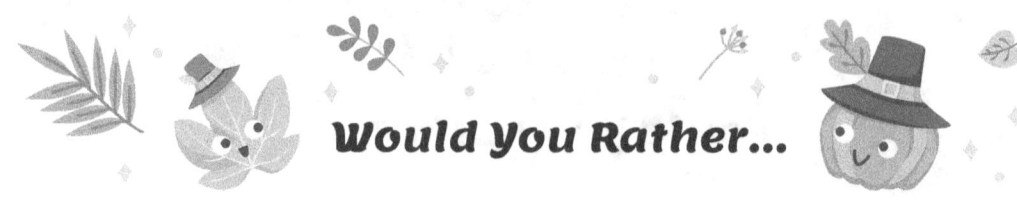

Have your grandpa fall asleep on your shoulder while watching the after-dinner football game

have to do the dishes with your grandma while she tells you all about knitting?

Eat extra crunchy roasted turkey-flavored potato chips

drink super fizzy cranberry-flavored soda?

 # Would You Rather...

Drizzle everything you eat with cinnamon caramel sauce

find pieces of hay in everything you eat for the whole month of October?

Play a game of backyard football using a buttered dinner roll

watch your favorite professional football team play a game using a buttered dinner roll?

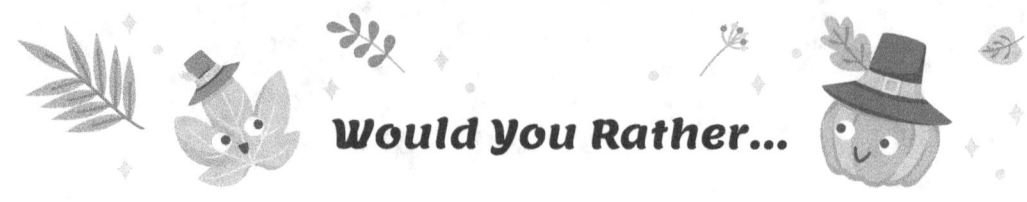

Would You Rather...

Have a scarecrow's itchy stiff straw for hair

be stuck on a pole in the middle of a cornfield like a real scarecrow for a day?

Sleep in a bed of musty smelling crunchy leaves

sleep curled up on top of a hay bale that makes you sneeze over and over?

Would you Rather...

Use a pumpkin pie flavored toothpaste for one week

eat an entire package of pumpkin pie flavored bubble gum in one day?

Go through a corn maze on a really dark night and have your flashlight batteries die

keep running into the same annoying and loud group of kids while going through the maze?

Would You Rather...

Be followed the whole way to school by a pack of curiously fluffy squirrels

try to eat a bowl full of acorns for lunch?

Hear the sound of crunchy leaves everywhere you walk

hear the sound of a really windy day in your ears all of the time?

 ## Would You Rather...

Dip your head into a bowl of melted caramel

create a school art sculpture using melted caramel?

Eat a peanut butter and jelly sandwich made with pumpkin bread

eat an apple butter and jelly sandwich on regular sandwich bread?

Would You Rather...

Have really bad fall allergies that make you sneeze five times every minute

get hiccups five times a day?

Be a fall tree that has really ugly colored wilted leaves

be a fall tree that drops all of its leaves in one day and is naked the rest of fall?

 # Would You Rather...

Spend a fall afternoon chopping logs wearing a red and black checkered shirt like a lumberjack

spend your fall afternoon dragging the heavy logs that a lumberjack chopped across a field to build a log cabin?

Play hide and seek in a hay bale maze

go bowling using pumpkins instead of bowling balls?

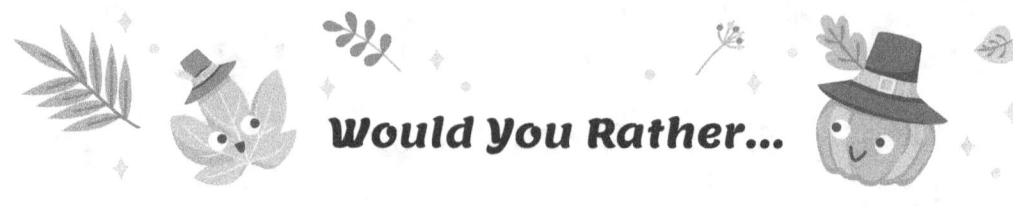

Would You Rather...

Have a scarecrow at your front door who seems to follow you with his eyes whenever you go in your house

a shifty scarecrow that mysteriously rides your school bus and always has a seat to himself?

Have everything you eat in autumn taste like sweet squashy fresh pumpkin

super sugary candy corns?

Would you Rather...

Accidentally wear your big pink bunny slippers instead of your sneakers to school

on pajama day find a big hole in the back of your pajamas that shows your underwear?

Finger paint with ruby red cranberries

stringy raw orange pumpkin guts?

Would You Rather...

Have your head turn into a big orange pumpkin with leafy vines for hair

a big red shiny apple with wormholes for eyes?

Wear a sweater that your cat unravels by pulling on a loose thread

knit a sweater as a gift for your mom that turns out to have one sleeve MUCH shorter than the other?

Would You Rather...

Scoop out a pumpkin for carving
with your tongue

wear the expression of your jack o'lantern
on your face for a week?

Go to an outdoor movie about crazy squirrels
in a park full of squirrels

watch an outdoor movie about crazy black crows in the
middle of a cornfield with a bunch of black crows?

Would You Rather...

Eat a whole pumpkin pie that is covered in ketchup

eat a whole apple pie that is covered in mustard?

Find leftover food scraps in the cafeteria and store them in a tree for later like a squirrel would

spend your days climbing up and down trees and hopping across fences like a squirrel?

Would You Rather...

Stand under a tree for an hour with apples that are constantly hitting you on the head

make applesauce by squishing apples in a tub with your toes?

Fall off the back of a hayride trailer while on a ride with your classmates

get your foot run over by the hayride trailer while you're trying to get on it?

Would You Rather...

Have a giant pumpkin to sit on instead of a desk chair

have an all-day gym class at a pumpkin patch where you have to roll giant pumpkins around the patch?

Eat a bowl of apple cinnamon oatmeal made from rotten apples

drink a glass of apple juice made from rotten apples?

 # Would You Rather...

Spend a week sitting in a bird's nest high up in a tree

spend a week dodging a bird that keeps dive bombing you every time you step outside?

Have a food fight in the cafeteria with mashed potatoes and gravy

creamy chocolate pudding?

Would You Rather...

Make a scarecrow out of straw
on a windy day

try to rake up all the fallen leaves in your yard
on a windy day?

Play on a playground where there are
wasps buzzing everywhere

on a playground that is totally buried
in crusty leaves?

 ## Would You Rather...

Be made of straw so you can never get hurt when you play dodgeball in gym class

have a squirrel's tail that you can use to play kickball in gym class?

Sit in a classroom all day that smells really strongly of pumpkin spice

sit in a classroom all day that smells really strongly of moldy leaves?

Would You Rather...

Spend all day climbing ladders to pick apples at an apple orchard

spend all day carrying around heavy pumpkins at a pumpkin patch?

Be able to shake cinnamon sugar out of your hair onto your food

pull apple cinnamon scented stickers off your tongue?

Would You Rather...

Eat an apple a day for the rest of your life

find an old apple core in your shoe every day for the rest of your life?

Eat a school cafeteria meal made only from squash

wear an outfit to school made entirely from dried corn husks?

 # Would You Rather...

Only be able to play video games after you've raked every single leaf from your yard

play a video game about being lost in a corn maze?

Play football when your hands are covered in slippery thick turkey gravy

when your hands are covered in sticky oozy caramel?

 ## Would You Rather...

Make all your food into
a giant Thanksgiving sandwich

find out there are no leftovers whatsoever after
the meal is over?

Eat a bowl of pumpkin pie flavored breakfast cereal

eat a bowl of your favorite breakfast cereal with pumpkin
pie flavored milk?

Would You Rather...

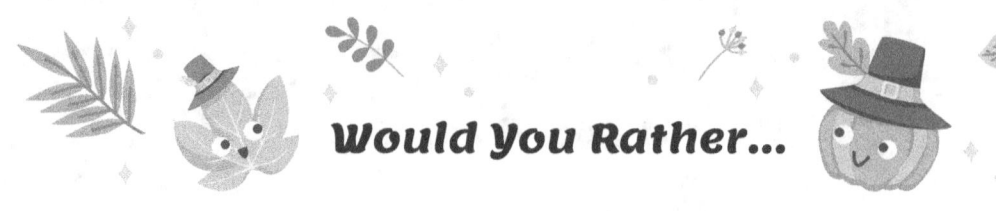

Eat turkey that is really chewy like beef jerky

mashed potatoes that are rubbery like a bowl of jello?

Get caught by your friends having your mom take your picture at the pumpkin patch

have to work cleaning up horse poo at the pumpkin patch's little kid pony ride?

 ## Would You Rather...

Have the cringy paper turkey you decorated in kindergarten displayed on your front door at Thanksgiving

have your photo taken wearing a cringy turkey costume on Thanksgiving Day every year?

Eat a bowl of applesauce that has been mushed by someone's feet

an apple pie that is made from hard and uncooked apples?

Would You Rather...

Dig potatoes out of your garden with a spoon for Thanksgiving dinner

comb your hair into a fancy style for the family gathering with a food-crusted fork?

Take your after-dinner-turkey-nap in a treehouse with creaky floorboards

snuggled up to your dog in his doghouse?

 # Would You Rather...

Eat a really yummy looking piece of pie that fell into your dirty kitchen sink

one that fell into the stuffed-full trash can?

Play a game of dodgeball in gym class using rotten apples that have fallen off a tree

tiny and really hard little acorns that you can throw by the handful?

Would You Rather...

Drink all the turkey roasting juices out of the pan

have to finish coloring a turkey placemat before you can eat dinner?

Snuggle up by the warm fire with a cup of hot apple juice that has spicy pepper in it instead of cinnamon

wear a cozy pair of slippers with giant holes in the toes that leave half your feet hanging out?

Would You Rather...

Be stuck on the sidelines as a cheerleader for the family football game

be stuck refereeing the game instead of playing?

Pour a ton of thick, brown, gravy on everything you eat for your Thanksgiving meal

drink a big ole' glass of brown gravy after stuffing your face on Thanksgiving?

Would You Rather...

Roll around in a pile of hay wearing only your swimsuit

dive into a giant dirty pit of dried up corn kernels?

Have a giant blowup turkey in the corner of your bedroom the week before Thanksgiving

wear a giant blowup turkey costume to school on the day before Thanksgiving?

 # Would You Rather...

Wear a crown made out of fallen pinecones that poke into your head

wear a hat made out of a hollowed out pumpkin shell that is still goopy inside?

Dig into a plateful of yams that turn out to be earwax

get passed your favorite dish of food right after your grandpa coughs all over it?

Would You Rather...

Chill out in front of the TV with a blanket and a moldy leaf scented candle

have to watch an hour long show on how to properly peel apples?

Have to find your way through a corn maze to get to the playground for recess

have your school cafeteria magically transported outside to picnic tables?

 ## Would You Rather...

Grow two very large front teeth like a squirrel and begin gnawing all of your food

become nocturnal like an owl and swoop down out of trees hunting mice at night?

Dress up like one of the original Pilgrims for Thanksgiving

eat your meal using only the utensils available to the first Pilgrims - spoons and knives, no forks?

Would You Rather...

Have a big black crow follow you wherever you go like a pet

have a squirrel decide to make its home in your backpack?

Eat deer or seafood for Thanksgiving like the first Pilgrims probably did

live in a log cabin that has no flushing toilets and only a fireplace for heat?

 ## Would You Rather...

Be a beautiful orange pumpkin covered with green warty looking bumps

an almost perfectly round orange pumpkin with a really big dent in it at the pumpkin patch?

Go to a school that has outhouses for bathrooms

a school that doesn't have pencil sharpeners?

Would You Rather...

Find a bunch of crunched up leaves
in your underwear

have a big clump of dried mud fall out
of your belly button?

Have to sit at the kiddie table with
a bunch of toddlers for dinner

get to sit at the adult table surrounded by your partly
deaf grandparents who can't hear what you say and yell
everything they say?

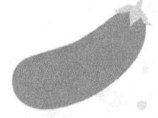  

 ## Would You Rather...

Get bounced off a hayride
into a big squishy mud puddle

step on a smelly rotten pumpkin
at the pumpkin patch?

Eat soup for every meal
in the months of September and October

eat a lettuce salad with cranberries and walnuts every day
during September and October?

Would You Rather...

Have crunchy green corn husks on your head instead of hair

drool melted caramel whenever you smell food?

Have to wear a bunch of stretched out hand-me-down sweaters from your cousin

have to take a super cheesy family photo where everyone wears a matching outfit and while you are taking the photo a bunch of your frenemies see you?

 # Would You Rather...

Drink a big cup of steaming hot chocolate out of a pumpkin shell

eat a steaming pile of cooked pumpkin drizzled with fudge sauce?

Spend your Friday night at a really boring football game that has no score after two hours

a really exciting football game, but mosquitos are eating you alive?

 ## Would You Rather...

Play a game of soccer with your friends using a pumpkin

play Marco Polo in a pool of apple juice?

Live in a warm place where the leaves stay green all year

live in a cool place where the leaves change to beautiful shades of red, orange, and gold?

Would You Rather...

Eat one meatloaf per day every day
for a month

sleep on top of a giant meatloaf for a week straight?

Go outside right after eating and play
a rowdy game of tackle football

watch a slideshow of embarrassing family pictures?

Would You Rather...

Eat a piece of pumpkin pie out of your sneaker

eat a piece of apple pie out of a dirty baseball cap?

Hide in a corn maze and scare kids walking by

get scared so bad by a kid hiding in the maze that you wet your pants?

Would You Rather...

Get hit in the face by an apple pie

have a giant container of applesauce dumped over your head?

Spend one hour a day for a year learning to knit

have to wear clothes to school that your mom has knitted for you?

Would You Rather...

Have the bushy tail of a squirrel that is always knocking things over

the painted-on face of a scarecrow that only shows one emotion?

Sail across the ocean on the Mayflower for 66 days like the Pilgrims

eat a full Thanksgiving meal once a day for 66 days straight?

Would You Rather...

Sleep overnight in a cave next to a warm fuzzy hibernating bear

come across a wide-awake bear while hiking in the woods?

Build a miniature log cabin using your green bean casserole

try to construct a perfect teepee by flattening your dinner roll and using your fork and spoon?

Would You Rather...

Eat a bowl of pumpkin soup that tastes like liquid earwax

eat a bowl of beet stew that tastes like dirt?

Tailgate at your favorite team's football game when it is only twenty degrees outside, and you're wrapped in a blanket shivering

tailgate in the hot baking sun on an eighty-five-degree day?

Would You Rather...

Swim ten laps across an Olympic-sized pool of apple cinnamon oatmeal

run five laps around a track that has a layer of slimy applesauce all over it?

Wear a shirt made entirely from super sweet orange, yellow, and white candy corns

made from faded, wrinkled, old Halloween candy wrappers?

Would You Rather...

Have a two-hour long conversation with a brainless scarecrow

the nerdiest person you know?

Find ants crawling all over the stick that you are roasting your marshmallow on

find ants crawling up the arm that you are holding your marshmallow stick with?

Would You Rather...

Have a tree climbing contest with a squirrel

a hole digging contest with your dog?

Work as the person who helps people find their way out of a corn maze

as the person who drives a hayride, doing the same circle over and over?

Did You Enjoy The Book?

If you did, we are ecstatic. If not, please write your complaint to us and we will ensure we fix it.

If you're feeling generous, there is something important that you can help me with – tell other people that you enjoyed the book.

Ask a grown-up to write about it on Amazon. When they do, more people will find out about the book. It also lets Amazon know that we are making kids around the world laugh. Even a few words and ratings would go a long way.

If you have any ideas or jokes that you think are super funny, please let us know. We would love to hear from you.

Our email address is -
riddleland@riddlelandforkids.com

Riddleland Bonus

Join our **Facebook Group** at **Riddleland for Kids** to get daily jokes and riddles.

https://pixelfy.me/riddlelandbonus

Thank you for buying this book. As a token of our appreciation, we would like to offer a special bonus—a collection of 50 original jokes, riddles, and funny stories.

CONTEST

Would you like your jokes and riddles to be featured in our next book?

We are having a contest to discover the cleverest and funniest boys and girls in the world!

1) Creative and Challenging Riddles
2) Tickle Your Funny Bone Contest

Parents, please email us your child's "original" riddle or joke. He or she could win a Riddleland book and be featured in our next book.

Here are the rules:

1) We're looking for super challenging riddles and extra funny jokes.

2) Jokes and riddles MUST be 100% original—NOT something discovered on the Internet.

3) You can submit both a joke and a riddle because they are two separate contests.

4) Don't get help from your parents—UNLESS they're as funny as you are.

5) Winners will be announced via email or our Facebook group – **Riddleland for kids**

6) In your entry, please confirm which book you purchased.

Email us at **Riddleland@riddlelandforkids.com**

Other Fun Books by Riddleland
Riddles Series

Would You Rather...Series

Get them on Amazon or our website at
www.riddlelandforkids.com

ABOUT RIDDLELAND

As parents, the biggest riddle we face is always, "Am I doing this parenting thing right?" Well, Riddleland is here to answer that question for you, and the answer is a resounding, "We have no idea because we're parents, too."

Riddleland believes that families are the most important thing in this world, and everything we do is for them. That's why we take extra care when creating innovative, fun, and age-appropriate concepts that help your kids think critically, enjoy reading, and simply be their wonderful selves. That's why we go above and beyond to support families by having many useful resources for kids, parents, and educators. And — most importantly — that's why we donate to support children and families in the U.S. and abroad, who don't have much access to fun and educational books, and why we only hire fellow, working-parents to help create our hilarious jokes, hand-drawn illustrations, mind-blowing trivia, and absurd would-you-rather questions that we double-dog dare you to read without laughing.

Pack up the kids (okay, not literally) and take a mental vacay to Riddleland to laugh, learn, and live in the moment.

If you have suggestions for us or want to work with us, shoot us an email at **riddleland@riddlelandforkids.com**

Our favourite family quote

"Creativity is an area in which younger people have a tremendous advantage since they have an endearing habit of always questioning past wisdom and authority."

– Bill Hewlett